KT-413-404

# JEROME
# BOSCH

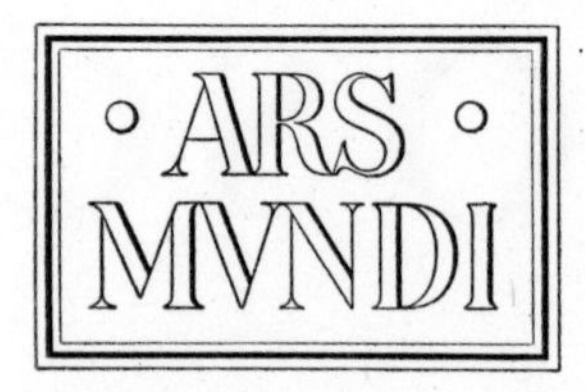


*Produced under the artistic direction of Jacques Lassaigne*

*Technical director Max Petitjean* (M.A P.)

# JEROME
# BOSCH

BY

F. M. GODFREY

LONDON

HOUSE OF BERIC LTD.

1, HIGH STREET MARYLEBONE W. 1.

JEROME BOSCH

*from the Collection of Portrait Paintings of Arras Library.*

JEROME Bosch (1450-1516), although a Flemish Primitive and a contemporary of Hugo van der Goes and Memling, was the first to abandon the traditional form of painting religious canvases for the use of the Church. He must have had a profoundly original mind and great strength of character, so to depart from the glorious conventions of his time which the brothers van Eyck, Roger van der Weyden, Dirck Bouts and a host of others had established, perpetuating in paint the celestial beauty of the Madonna or the moving drama of the Lord's Passion, the angelic host and the saintly denizens of the apostolic age. Bosch, who came from the Gothic city of's Hertogenbosch, was in fact untouched by the Renaissance ideal of terrestrial beauty in which the van Eycks and their followers were clothing the world of appearances. He was at heart a medievalist whose Gothic imagination abounded in nightmare-visions of satanic propensity. Carel van Mander, his first biographer, simply says "he painted gruesome pictures of spooks and horrid phantoms of Hell."

At home he was a member of the religious brotherhood of Our Lady. This must have been a puritanical association, a community of reformers before the Reformation, haunted by fear and bent upon the cleansing of body and soul, particularly among the members of the Church. In his four great canvases where sinful man is shown in all conditions of crime and punishment — the *Haywaggon*, the *Garden of Delight*, the *Last Judgment*, *The Temptation of St. Anthony* — nuns and monks play a conspicuous part. Bosch must have been a witness of terrible crimes and cruelties, of plague and torture and abnormal vice, which his insatiable fancy absorbed and then splattered upon his canvas in an orgy of incoherent imagery. That character of his crowded mosaics, representing human vice and folly in the raw followed by instantaneous retribution, has led some interpreters to find sur-realist elements in Bosch's utterances. That is not surprising. For all communion with the transcendental realm must use a language of super-natural symbolism in order to express the internal experience. Moreover, for Bosch as for all medieval men, Hell and Purgatory and Paradise were a living reality and the infernal machinery, the penalties suffered, the demons that inhabited the sulphurous place fired the imagination of the artist to his bold and novel abstractions.

A Spanish monk, Joseph de Siguenca, who catalogued Bosch's paintings for his infatuated royal master and connoisseur, King Philip II, has admirably summed up the case by saying that the difference between Bosch's painting and that of others lies in the fact that the others aspired to paint " man as he is externally, only he (Bosch) had the audacity to paint the inner man. " His genius lay in the fact that the " inner man " was revealed to him, although he concentrated upon the infernal distortions and not on the natural grace of man. While in his long and active life he painted three great canvases of the *Adoration* and endowed several of his pictures with superb landscape-backgrounds whose influence will be felt in the works of Brueghel and of Patinir, all his personal effort went towards the expression of the phantastical, the gruesome, the vicious and the malign. Even if he paints the Passion of Christ, it is not spiritual strength or saintly martyrdom which is his real subject, but the abject mockery, vile cruelty and primitive hate which His tormentors display.

" The world is a mound of hay, each one takes what he can grasp ", says an old Flemish proverb which inspired Bosch's phantasy of the *Haywaggon*, now in the Escorial. It is the image of earthly vanity. On an enormous chariot of hay which passes through a beautiful river-valley is a group of young lovers. All humanity, monks, burghers, peasants, Pope, Emperor and Princes follow in its train, hang on to its load or are crushed under its wheels. Drawn by demons the chariot passes on its irrevocable way to Hell. Inferno is placed in a burning landscape where sinful men are crossing a bridge to the city of Dis, goaded and assailed by monsters. On the left panel is depicted the Fall of Adam and Eve.

The second great triptych of Bosch is *The Temptation of St. Anthony*, painted in the last decade of the 15th century and now in the Museum of Lisbon. It has been said that the famous contemporary treatise on sorcerers, magicians and witches, the *Malleus Maleficarum* of 1487, determined the painter to surround the hermit with the unspeakable horrors and configurations of this sect. They invade his solitude, they travel through the air, they celebrate the "black mass", they threaten with monstrous shapes and weapons — dragon, frog and sow-headed creatures — the retreat of the haunted man. This nocturne, this witches' sabbath with its sexual symbolism must be the most perfect impersonation of the Satanic in pictorial art.

But the consummation of Bosch's phantasy, the extreme and psycho-analytical symbolism of his invention must be studied in the so-called *Garden of Delight*, a three-tiered maze of human nudes, monstrous animals, birds and fishes, aquatic plants, giant flowers and fruit. Graceful, idyllic figures of men and women, apparently innocent, enjoy one another and the luxuriant gifts of the earth. But in the middle distance an unrelenting dance of the passions takes place around the fountain of youth, where men and beasts eternally circle in a wild and senseless orgy of desire. Above it, the pond of luxury with monstrous flowers and rocks, where the adulterers and other carnal sinners complete the Divine Comedy of human vanity. The Earthly Paradise and again the Infernal City surround the Garden of Delight on either side. Bosch composes here "a symphony of machines of vengeance" where the abstract and disjointed symbolism of form approaches an unbearable and morbid character of hallucination. It is as if all the accumulated poison and capacity for evil of the whole human race had been diverted into the psychopathic superstructure which Jerome Bosch distilled from the residue of the Dark Ages.

It is the riot of sublunary form in the Escorial triptych which transcends in a complete sur-realist vision where all created things appear in phantastic distortion and dismemberment. In contemplating the uncanny face that looks at you from underneath a semi-human tree, the giant pair of ears pierced by the shaft of a lance or the nude suspended on a harp, acrobats in a transparent bowl of steel, the human bat or the human mollusc — this disconnected and self-analytical nightmare of medieval man becomes strangely relevant and almost contemporary. But the extremities of this dream-creation apart, Bosch has reached a rare technical mastery, a rare purity of tints and glazes where gold and crystal and glass and the pearly flesh tones of the human body shine in a lustrous and smooth transparency.

Bosch is above all an illustrator, a narrator who fascinates more by the contents of his story than by his consummate artistry. He was no portraitist. The plastic three-dimensional form of the human body did not interest him. He was an eminently lineal artist whose form of expression is outline, profile, silhouette. A mind so haunted by spirits, a brain so seething with apparition could hardly be expected to marshal its resources, and his crowded canvases abound in masses of figures and bizarre contractions, incomprehensible at times, without order and symmetry, diabolic, eccentric and irregular.

He was only interested in caricature. The Pure and the Saintly often show an insensible smile while all the cunning and shrewdness are concentrated upon the Vicious. Even the Saint for Bosch is above all a being to be tempted, mocked and assaulted by the infernal hordes. St. Anthony sits and gazes into the distance while Lucifer's host approaches with ingenious machines of war. Similarly St. Jerome lies in penance on the ground, exposed to "an insidious Fauna and Flora," ready to loose its devilish spook upon the Saint.

With a complete indifference to the forms and creations of nature, propelled by his gloomy and satirical view of man, Bosch denies the borders between man and beast and satanically mixes their attributes. Thus he peoples his infernal regions with a revolting host of monsters and demons and reveals humanity in their abysmal pursuit of lust and of greed. Yet among his several conceptions of the Infernal City, his elaborate *Temptations of St. Jerome* and *St. Anthony*, his superb *St. Christopher*, set against a magnificent river-landscape — also haunted by gibbets and uncanny tree-forms which reveal a phantastic vitality — Bosch has painted one picture of the greatest personal and spiritual significance.

The *Return of the Prodigal Son* at the Boymans Museum in Rotterdam is without doubt the most self-revealing and the most melancholy picture that Jerome Bosch has ever painted. He does not show the prodigal son in the embrace of the forgiving father, welcomed and admired by kith and kin, but has chosen the moment of the greatest psychological impact where the returning wanderer must make the decision between the good life and the bad. His lean ragged figure is shown in motion. His wounded leg, the weight of his body, his arm thrust forward, his hat with the cobbler's awl point towards the paternal gate, but the man himself, tall, haggard, prematurely aged, looks back over his shoulder to the tumble-down tavern which he leaves behind, with all the misery, the vice, the wretchedness that the wayside inn embodies for the impecunious traveller.

The prodigal son, as he looms large in front of the paternal gate that he will enter in spite of conflicting desires, is perhaps the first psychological portrait in the whole history of painting. This face is unforgettable, wistful, melancholy, profound, possessed, the image of a soul forlorn in a world " where there is no God. " Behind this fated apparition we behold the homely meadows, the flowering tree, the gate and cow. Against this the painter has set a genre picture of the utmost dilapidation, the Inn of the Jug and Swan with broken windows and crumbling roof, where man and beast seem equally wretched. The grey and silver tones of fields and sky are in harmony with the grey rags of the prodigal son, who lightly carries his basket towards a better life which his disillusioned eye hardly foresees. Was this the way the painter Jerome Bosch looked upon the world ? The evidence of his work seems to support this view.

F. M. G.

# LIST OF ILLUSTRATIONS

30. THE HAY WAGGON, *detail of centre panel:* PAIRS OF LOVERS.
31. THE HAY WAGGON, *detail of centre panel:* CAVALCADE OF THE GREAT—BISHOP, EMPEROR, KING.
32. THE HAY WAGGON, *detail of left volet:* ADAM AND EVE.
33. THE HAY WAGGON, *detail of right volet:* CAVALCADE OF DEMONS.
34. THE CARRYING OF THE CROSS: h. 59"; w. 37". Escorial, Madrid. (Vernacci.)
35. THE CARRYING OF THE CROSS: h. 22"; w. 12 ½". Kunsthistorisches Museum, Vienna. (Wolfrum.)
36. THE CARRYING OF THE CROSS, *reverse*: THE INFANT JESUS. (Wolfrum.)
37. THE LAST JUDGMENT, *reverse of volets, each volet:* h. 66"; w. 24". *Left volet*: ST. JAMES OF COMPOSTELLA. *Right volet*: ST. BAVON.
38. THE LAST JUDGMENT, *centre panel*: h. 64"; w. 50". Fine Arts Academy, Vienna.
39. THE LAST JUDGMENT, *left volet*: THE EARTHLY PARADISE; *right volet:* HELL. *Each volet:* h. 66"; w. 24".
40. THE WORLD AFTER THE DELUGE: THE DELUGE (*forming a diptych with* HELL): h. 27"; w. 15". Boymans Museum, Rotterdam. (Boymans.)
41. THE WORLD AFTER THE DELUGE, *reverse of* THE DELUGE: BIBLICAL PARABLES. (Boymans.)
42. THE WORLD AFTER THE DELUGE: HELL (*forming a diptych with* THE DELUGE). (Boymans.)
43. THE WORLD AFTER THE DELUGE, *reverse of* HELL: BIBLICAL PARABLES. (Boymans.)
44. HELL—THE FALL OF THE DAMNED, *each panel*: h. 34"; w. 16". Doges' Palace, Venice. (Vernacci.)
45. PARADISE—THE ASCENT TOWARDS PARADISE, *each panel:* h. 34"; w. 16". (Anderson.)
46. ECCE HOMO: h. 20"; w. 21". Johnson Collection, Philadelphia. (By courtesy of.)
47. THE TEMPTATION OF ST. ANTHONY, *volets closed, each*: h. 52"; w. 20". *Left volet:* ARREST OF CHRIST. *Right volet:* CARRYING THE CROSS. National Fine Arts Museum, Lisbon. (Laboratoire Musée du Louvre.)
48. THE TEMPTATION OF ST. ANTHONY, *centre panel*: h. 52" w. 46". (Laboratoire Musée du Louvre.)
49. THE TEMPTATION OF ST. ANTHONY, *volets open*; *left volet*: THE SWOONING OF ST. ANTHONY. *Right volet:* THE TEMPTATION OF THE FLESH. (Laboratoire Musée du Louvre.)
50. THE TEMPTATION OF ST. ANTHONY, *detail of closed left volet*: THE EPISODE OF MALCHUS.
51. THE TEMPTATION OF ST. ANTHONY, *detail of closed right volet*: THE CONFESSION OF THE GOOD THIEF.
52. THE TEMPTATION OF ST. ANTHONY, *detail of closed right volet:* MONK EXHORTING THE WICKED THIEF.

53. THE TEMPTATION OF ST. ANTHONY, *detail of centre panel:* HEAD AND HANDS OF A DEMON.
54. THE TEMPTATION OF ST. ANTHONY, *detail of centre panel:* DEMONIAC RIDER.
55. THE TEMPTATION OF ST. ANTHONY, *detail of centre panel:* THE SAINT TEMPTED.
56. THE TEMPTATION OF ST. ANTHONY, *detail of open left volet:* THE SAINT SWOONING.
57. THE TEMPTATION OF ST. ANTHONY, *detail of open left volet:* HEAD OF A LAYMAN BEARING ST. ANTHONY.
58. THE TEMPTATION OF ST. ANTHONY, *detail of open left volet:* ST. ANTHONY RAISED FROM THE GROUND BY DEMONS.
59. THE TEMPTATION OF ST. ANTHONY, *detail of open left volet:* THE WORLD IN THE PREY OF DEMONS.
60. THE TEMPTATION OF ST. ANTHONY, *detail of open right volet*: THE MAGIC TABLE.
61. ST. JOHN THE BAPTIST IN THE DESERT: h. 19"; w. 16". Boymans Museum (private collection), Rotterdam.
63. THE GARDEN OF DELIGHT, *volets closed*: THE CREATION OF THE WORLD: h. 86"; w. 77". Prado, Madrid. (Mas.)
64. THE GARDEN OF DELIGHT, *centre panel*: h. 86"; w. 77". (Anderson.)
65. THE GARDEN OF DELIGHT, *volets open. Left*: PARADISE; *Right*: HELL. (Anderson.)
66. THE GARDEN OF DELIGHT, *detail of centre panel:* MINERAL PROLIFERATION.
67. THE GARDEN OF DELIGHT, *detail of centre panel.*
68. THE GARDEN OF DELIGHT, *detail of centre panel:* THE FOUNTAIN OF YOUTH.
69. THE GARDEN OF DELIGHT, *detail of open left volet:* THE ANIMAL OF PARADISE.
70. THE GARDEN OF DELIGHT, *detail of open right volet:* THE BAGPIPES.
71. THE GARDEN OF DELIGHT, *detail of open right volet:* DEMONIAC AMUSEMENTS.
72. RETABLE OF ST. JULIA, *centre panel:* THE MARTYRDOM OF THE SAINT: h. 40"; w. 25". Doges' Palace, Venice. (Alinari.)
73. RETABLE OF ST. JULIA, *volets open. Left:* TEMPTATION OF ST. ANTHONY. *Right:* SLAVE MERCHANTS. *Each volet:* h. 40", w. 11". (Alinari.)
74. RETABLE OF THE HERMITS, *centre panel:* ST. JEROME AT PRAYER: h. 34"; w. 24". Doges' Palace, Venice. (Alinari.)
75. RETABLE OF THE HERMITS, *volets open. Left:* TEMPTATION OF ST. ANTHONY. *Right:* ST. GILES AT PRAYER. *Each volet:* h. 34"; w. 11 1/2". (Alinari.)

76. ST. JOHN IN PATMOS : h. 24"; w. 16. Deutsches Museum, Berlin. (Museum.)
77. ST. JOHN IN PATMOS, *reverse :* THE PASSION OF CHRIST. (Museum.)
78. ST. JOHN IN PATMOS, *detail :* LANDSCAPE.
79. ST. JOHN IN PATMOS, *detail of reverse :* CALVARY.
80. ST. JEROME AT PRAYER : h. 30"; w. 23". Musée des Beaux-Arts. Ghent.
81. ST. CHRISTOPHER : h. 45"; w. 28". Boymans Museum, Rotterdam.
83. THE EPIPHANY, *volets closed* : ST. GREGORY'S MASS : h. 54" ; w. 28". Prado, Madrid. (Vernacci.)
84. THE EPIPHANY, *centre panel.* (Anderson.)
85. THE EPIPHANY, *volets open. Left :* THE DONOR AND ST. PETER. *Right :* THE DONOR'S WIFE AND ST. AGNES. *Each volet :* h. 54" ; w. 13". (Anderson.)
86. THE EPIPHANY, *detail of centre panel :* GROUP FROM THE ADORATION.
87. THE EPIPHANY, *detail of centre panel :* YOUNG NEGRO ASSISTING BALTHAZAR.
88. THE EPIPHANY, *volets closed* : h. 23" ; w. 10", ST. PETER'S CH., Brussels. *Left volet :* ST. PETER. *Right volet :* MARY MAGDALENE.
89. THE EPIPHANY, *centre panel :* THE ADORATION OF THE MAGI. (Boymans.)
90. THE EPIPHANY, *volets open. Left :* ST. JOSEPH. *Right :* THE SUITE OF THE MAGI. (Boymans.)
91. THE CROWNING WITH THORNS : H. 65" ; w. 77". Prado, Madrid. (Anderson.)
92. THE CROWNING WITH THORNS : h. 33 1/2" ; w. 27". Museum of Antwerp (after an original by Jerome Bosch). (J. t' Felt.)
93. THE CROWNING WITH THORNS : h. 29" ; w. 23". National Gallery, London. (Tisné.)
94. CHRIST BEFORE PILATE : h. 33 1/2" ; w. Princeton Art Museum, New Jersey. (By courtesy of.)
95. CHRIST BEFORE PILATE, *detail.*
96. THE CARRYING OF THE CROSS : h. 29" ; w. 32". Musée des Beaux-Arts, Ghent. (Archives Photo.)
97. THE CARRYING OF THE CROSS, *detail :* VERONICA AND CHRIST. CHRIST (Tisné.)
99. THE TEMPTATION OF ST. ANTHONY : h. 28" ; w. 20". Prado, Madrid.
100. THE PRODIGAL SON, diam. 28". Boymans Museum, Rotterdam. (Boymans.)
101. THE PRODIGAL SON, *detail :* THE PRODIGAL.
102. THE PRODIGAL SON, *detail :* THE SWAN INN.

ON THE JACKET : THE CONJURER, *detail.* Municipal Museum, Saint-Germain-en-Laye.

# BIBLIOGRAPHY

M. G. GOSSART — *JEROME BOSCH*. Lille, 1907.

PAUL LAFOND — *HIERONIMUS BOSCH*. Brussels, 1914.

W. SCHURMEYER — *HIERONIMUS BOSCH*. Munich, 1923.

D. HANNEMA et G. VAN GELDER — *CATALOGUE OF THE JEROME BOSCH EXHIBITION*. Rotterdam, 1936.

A. CHASTEL — *LA TENTATION DE SAINT ANTOINE ou LE SONGE DU MELANCOLIQUE*. G. B. A., 1936.

C. DE TOLNAY — *HIERONIMUS BOSCH*. Basle, 1937.

J. DUPONT — *JEROME BOSCH : LE RETABLE DE SAINT-ANTOINE*. Paris, 1937.

M. BRION — *BOSCH*. Paris, 1938.

M. J. FRIEDLANDER — *HIERONIMUS BOSCH*. The Hague, 1941.

L. VON BALDASS — *H. BOSCH*. Vienna, 1941.

L. PARROT — *LA FLAMME ET LA CENDRE ; FORMES ET COULEURS*. 1944.

L. VAN DEN BOSSCHE — *JEROEN BOSCH*. Diest, 1944.

J. COMBE — *JEROME BOSCH*. Paris, 1946.

H. DANIEL — *HIERONIMUS BOSCH*. Paris, 1947.

J. DE BOSCHERE — *JEROME BOSCH*. Brussels, 1947.

P. FIERENS — *LE FANTASTIQUE DANS L'ART FLAMAND*. Brussels, 1947.

# PLATES

THE CURING OF MADNESS.

THE CARDINAL SINS, *detail :* BEWARE, GOD SEES.

4 THE CARDINAL SINS, *detail:* THE DEATH OF THE SINNER — HEL

THE CARDINAL SINS, *detail :* THE LAST JUDGMENT. — PARADISE.

6 THE CARDINAL SINS, *detail:* AVARICE

THE CARDINAL SINS, *detail:* ENVY.

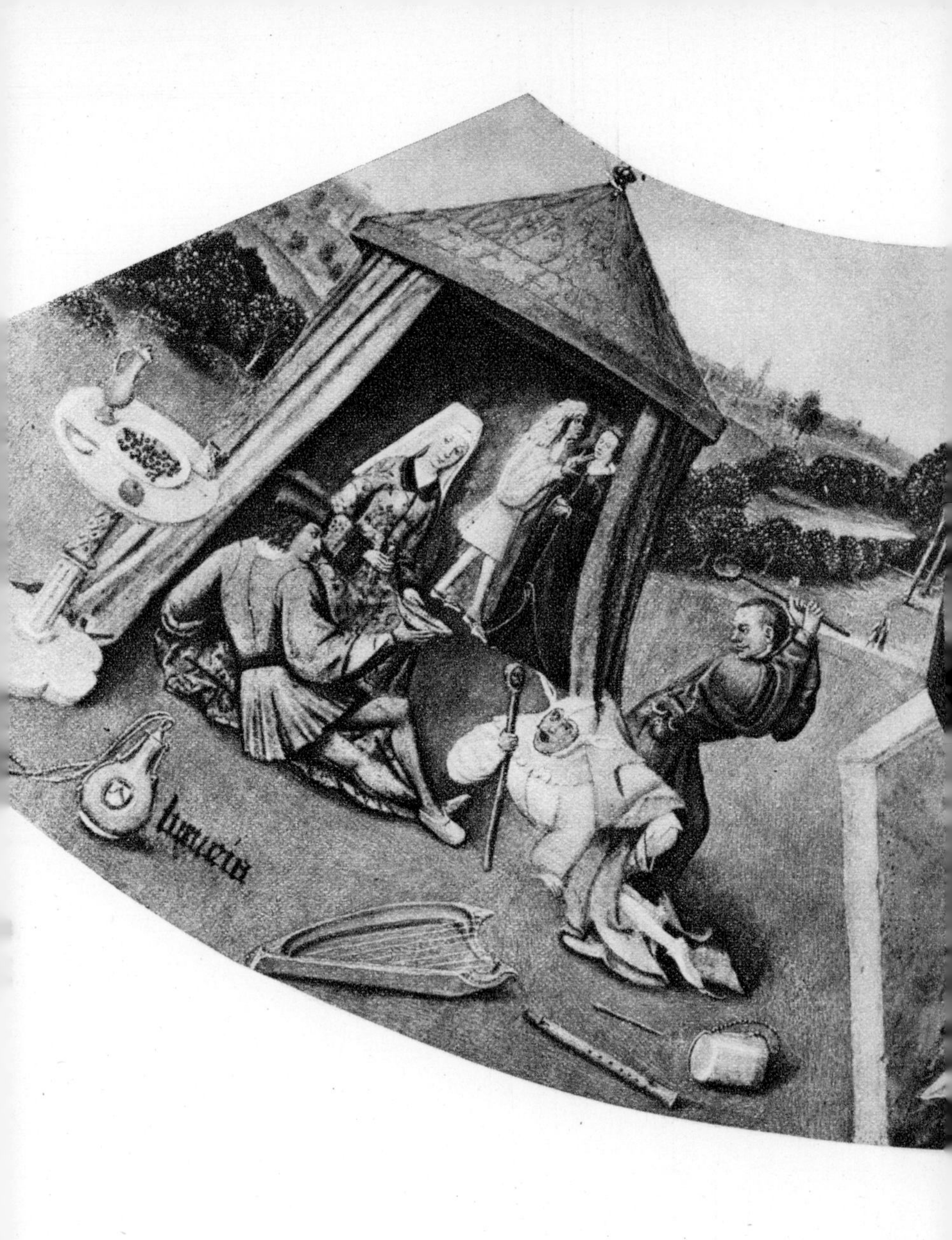



THE CARDINAL SINS, *detail:* LECHERY.

THE CARDINAL SINS, *detail:* SLOTH.

THE CARDINAL SINS, *detail:* GLUTTONY

THE EPIPHANY.

12 ECCE HOMO.

ECCE HOMO, *detail:* CHRIST AND HIS EXECUTIONERS.

CHRIST ON THE CROSS

CHRIST ON THE CROSS, *detail:* THE VIRGIN AND ST. JOHN.

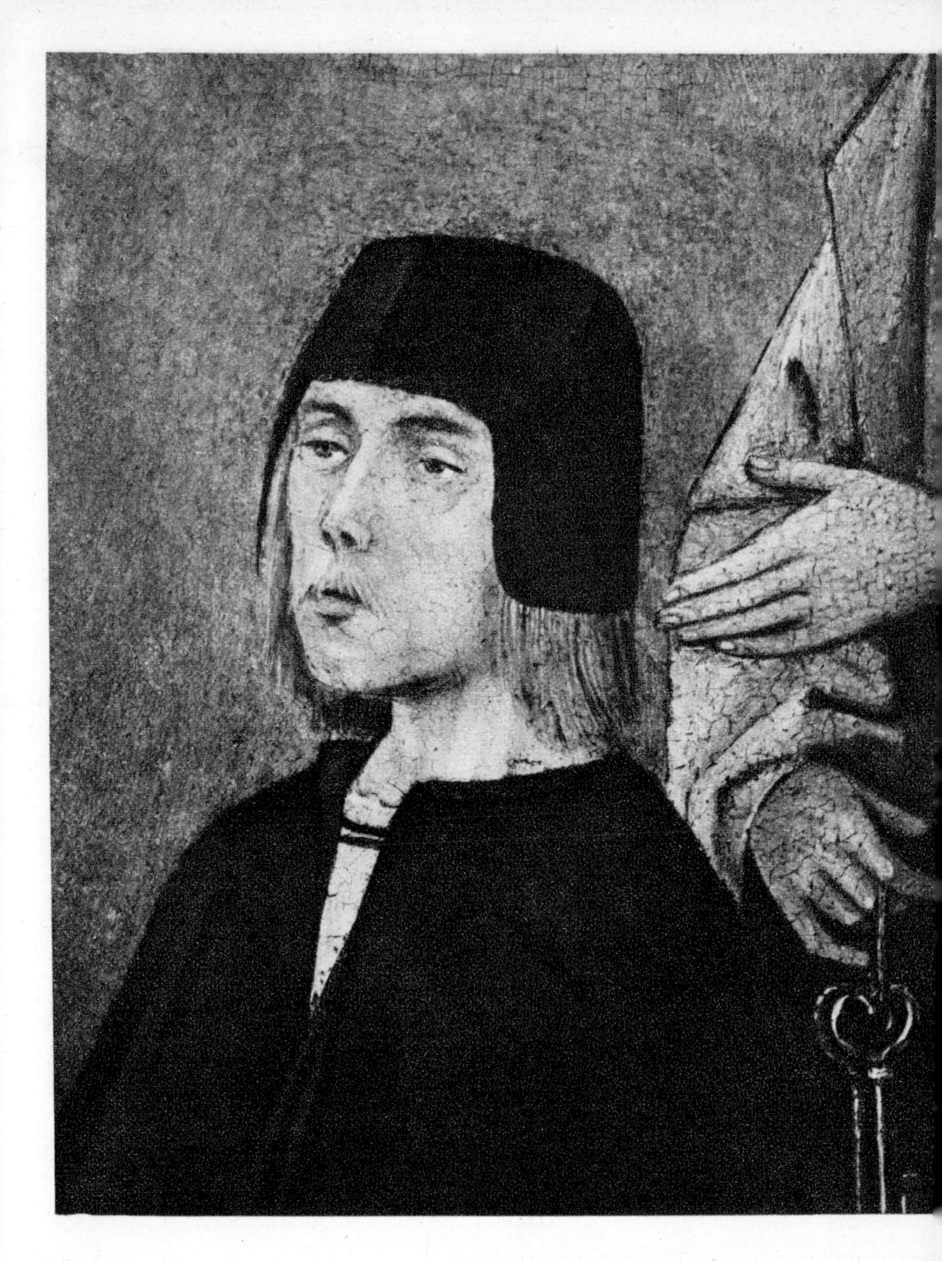



CHRIST ON THE CROSS, *detail* : THE DONOI

THE WEDDING FEAST OF CANA, *detail :* THE BETROTHED.

HE WEDDING FEAST OF CANA.

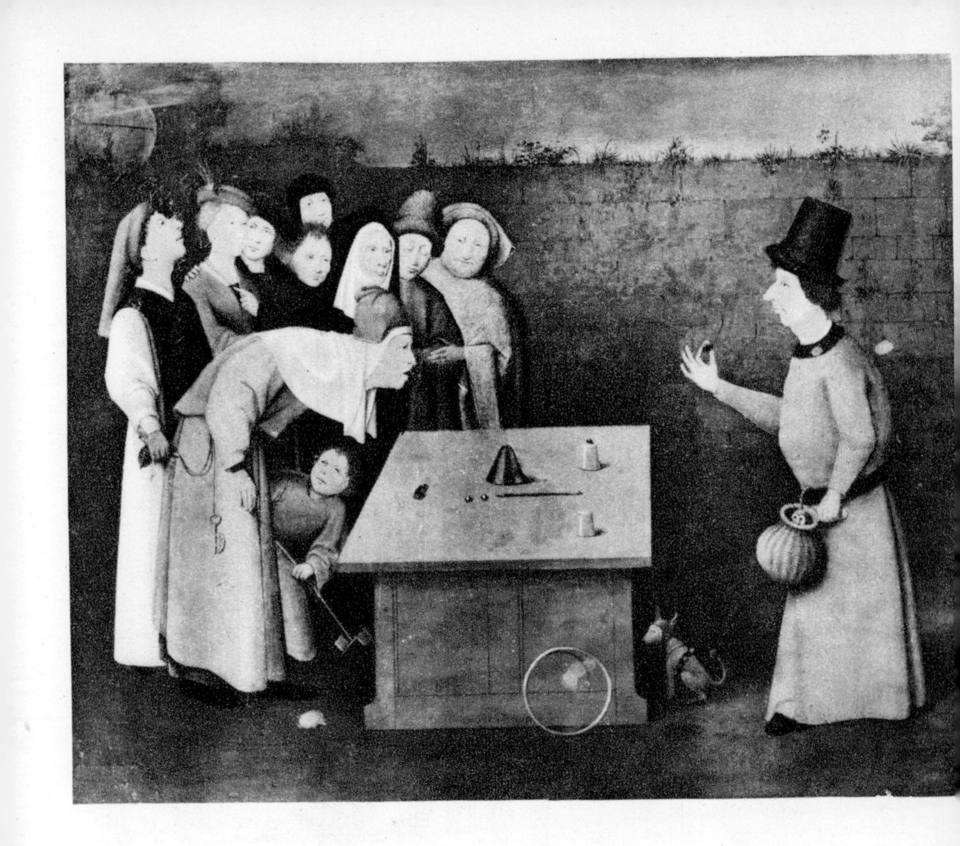



THE CONJURER

THE SHIP OF FOOLS.

THE DEATH OF THE MISER.

THE HAY WAGGON. Triptych (closed) : THE WANDERING FOOL.

THE HAY WAGGON, *centre panel.*

THE HAY WAGGON, *left volet :* THE EARTHLY PARADISE. *Right volet :* HELL.

THE HAY WAGGON, *detail of the closed triptych:* THIEVES PLUNDERING A PASSER-BY.

THE HAY WAGGON, *detail of centre panel:* BRAWL BETWEEN THE WHEELS OF THE WAGGON. 27.

THE HAY WAGGON, *detail of centre panel:* MONK DRINKING AND NUNS.

30 THE HAY WAGGON, *detail of centre panel:* PAIRS OF LOVERS

HE HAY WAGGON, *detail of centre panel:* CAVALCADE OF THE GREAT—BISHOP, EMPEROR, KING.

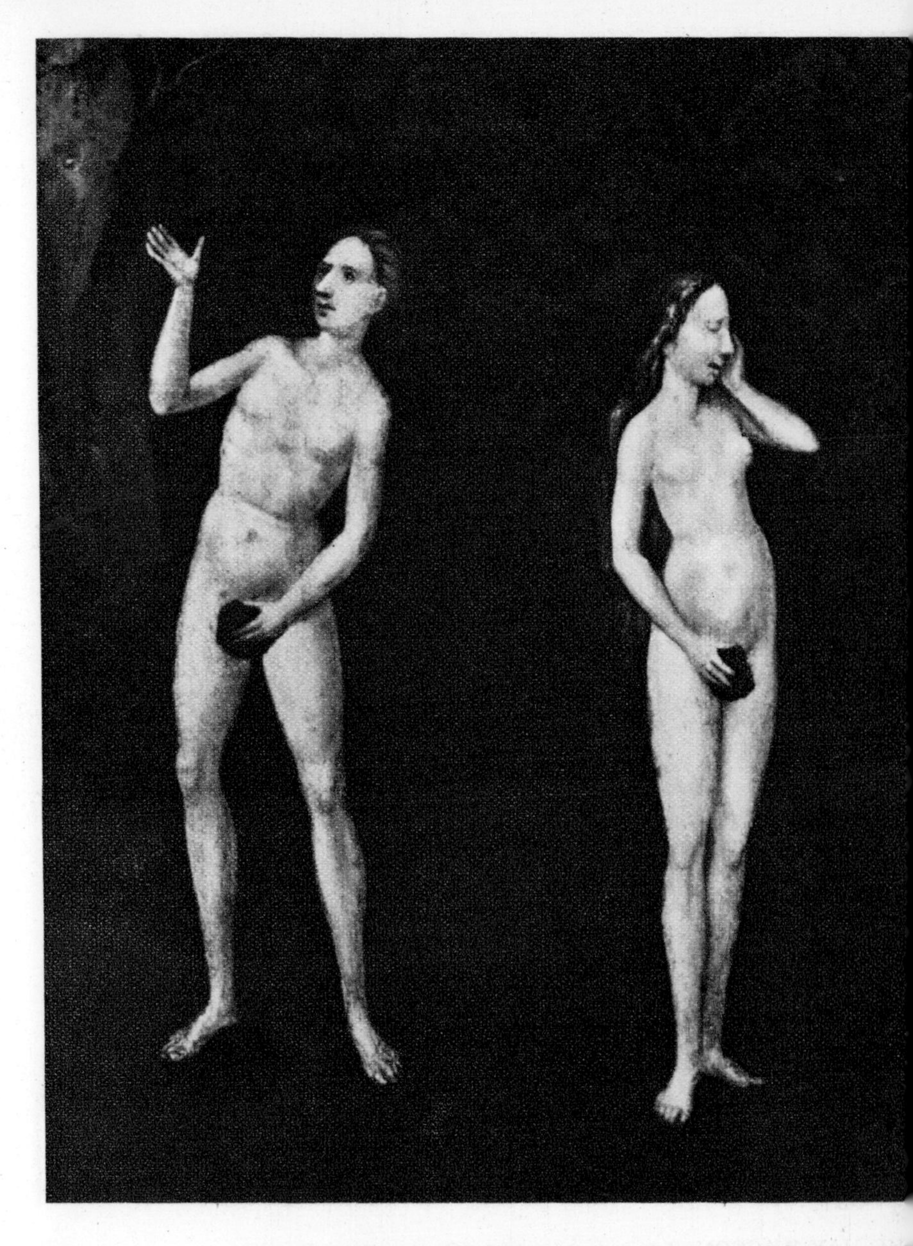



THE HAY WAGGON, *detail of left volet :* ADAM AND E

HE HAY WAGGON, *detail of right volet :* CAVALCADE OF DEMONS.

THE CARRYING OF THE CROS

HE CARRYING OF THE CROSS.

36 THE CARRYING OF THE CROSS, *reverse:* THE INFANT JESUS.

HE LAST JUDGMENT, *reverse of volets. Left volet:* ST. JAMES OF COMPOSTELLA. *Right volet:* ST. BAVON.

THE LAST JUDGMENT, *centre pan*

'HE LAST JUDGMENT, *left volet :* THE EARTHLY PARADISE ; *right volet :* HELL.

THE WORLD AFTER THE DELUGE : THE DELUG
*(forming a diptych with* HELL*).*

THE WORLD AFTER THE DELUGE, *reverse of* THE DELUGE: BIBLICAL PARABLES.

THE WORLD AFTER THE DELUGE : HELL
*(forming a diptych with* THE DELUGE).

IE WORLD AFTER THE DELUGE, *reverse of* HELL : BIBLICAL PARABLES.

HELL—THE FALL OF THE DAMNE

PARADISE—THE ASCENT TOWARDS PARADISE.

ECCE HOMO.

HE TEMPTATION OF ST. ANTHONY, *volets closed. Left volet:* ARREST OF CHRIST. *Right volet:* CARRYING THE CROSS.

THE TEMPTATION OF ST. ANTHONY, *centre pane*

THE TEMPTATION OF ST. ANTHONY, *volets open ; left volet :* THE SWOONING OF ST. ANTHONY. *Right volet :* THE TEMPTATION OF THE FLESH.

50 THE TEMPTATION OF ST. ANTHONY, *detail of closed left volet*
THE EPISODE OF MALCHUS.

THE TEMPTATION OF ST. ANTHONY, *detail of closed right volet:* THE CONFESSION OF THE GOOD THIEF.

52 THE TEMPTATION OF ST. ANTHONY, *detail of closed right volet:* MONK EXHORTING THE WICKED THIEF.

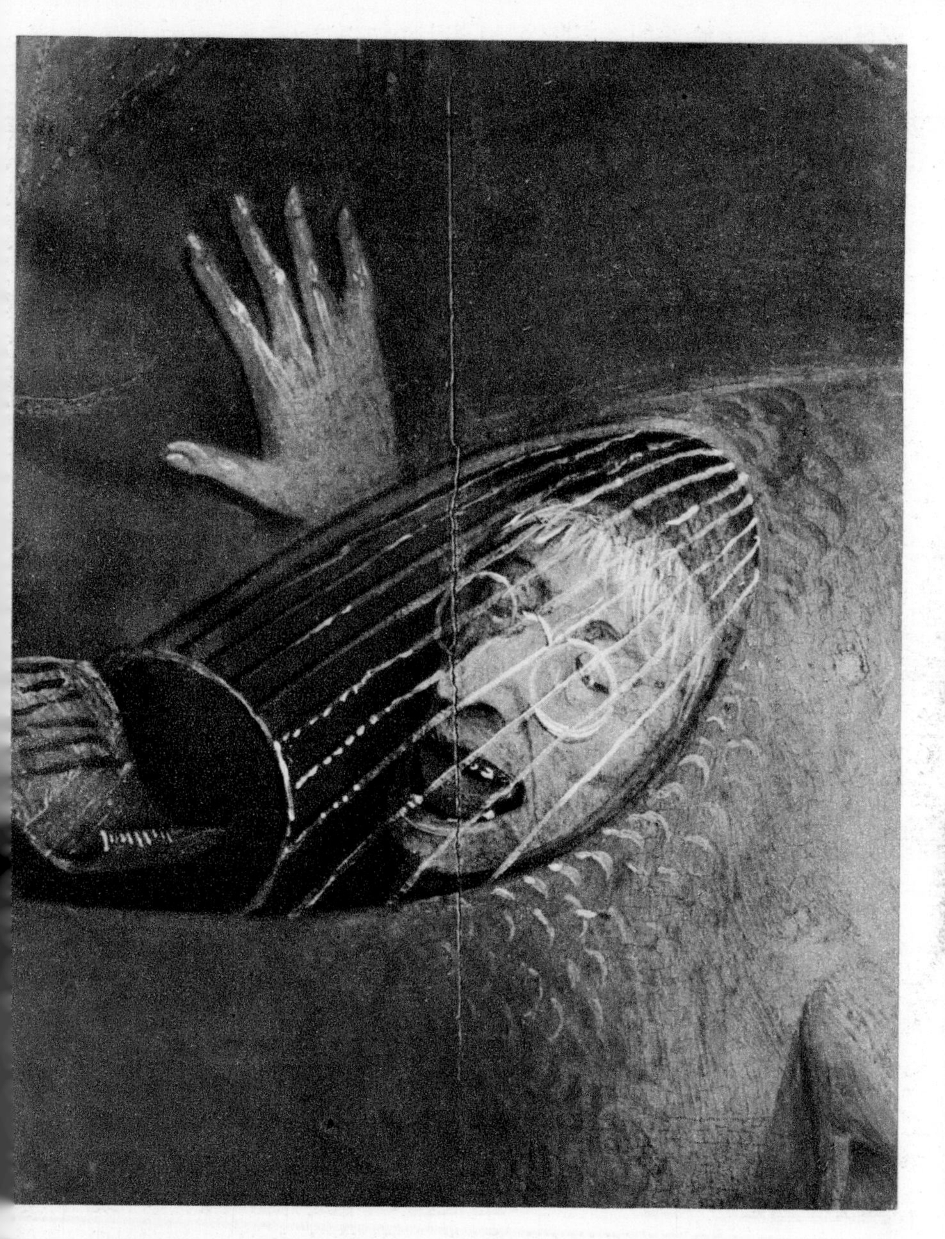

'HE TEMPTATION OF ST. ANTHONY, *detail of centre panel:*
HEAD AND HANDS OF A DEMON.

THE TEMPTATION OF ST. ANTHONY, *detail of centre pane*
DEMONIAC RIDER.

THE TEMPTATION OF ST. ANTHONY, *detail of centre panel:* THE SAINT TEMPTED.

56 THE TEMPTATION OF ST. ANTHONY, *detail of open left volet*
THE SAINT SWOONING.

IE TEMPTATION OF ST. ANTHONY, *detail of open left volet:*
IEAD OF A LAYMAN BEARING ST. ANTHONY.

THE TEMPTATION OF ST. ANTHONY, *detail of open left vol*
THE WORLD IN THE PREY OF DEMONS.

THE TEMPTATION OF ST. ANTHONY, *detail of open left volet:*
THE WORLD IN THE PREY OF DEMONS.

60 THE TEMPTATION OF ST. ANTHONY, *detail of open right volet:* THE MAGIC TABLE.

ST. JOHN THE BAPTIST IN THE DESERT.

THE GARDEN OF DELIGHT, *volets closed :* THE CREATION OF THE WORLD.

THE GARDEN OF DELIGHT, *centre panel.*

THE GARDEN OF DELIGHT, *volets open. Left:* PARADISE; *Right:* HELL.

66 THE GARDEN OF DELIGHT, *detail of centre panel:* MINERAL PROLIFERATION.

THE GARDEN OF DELIGHT, *detail of centre panel.*

68 THE GARDEN OF DELIGHT, *detail of centre panel:* THE FOUNTAIN OF YOUTH.

THE GARDEN OF DELIGHT, *detail of open left volet:* THE ANIMAL OF PARADISE.

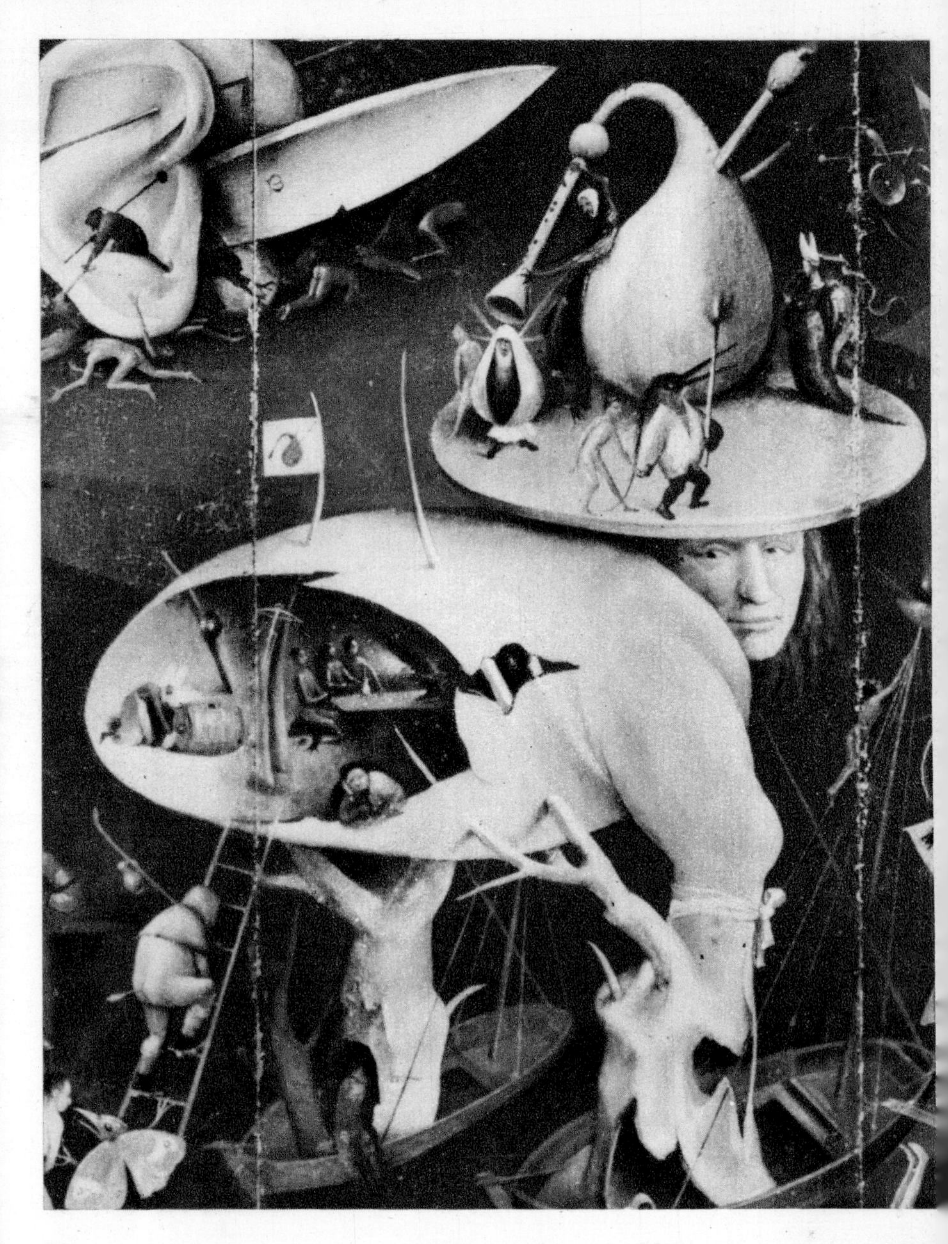

 THE GARDEN OF DELIGHT, *detail of open right volet:* THE BAGPIPES.

THE GARDEN OF DELIGHT, *detail of open right volet:* DEMONIAC AMUSEMENTS.

RETABLE OF ST. JULIA, *centre panel:* THE MARTYRDOM OF THE SAINT

ETABLE OF ST. JULIA, *volets open. Left :* TEMPTATION OF ST. ANTHONY.
*Right :* SLAVE MERCHANTS.

 RETABLE OF THE HERMITS, *centre panel:* ST. JEROME AT PRAYER

RETABLE OF THE HERMITS, *volets open. Left :* TEMPTATION OF ST. ANTHONY.
*Right :* ST. GILES AT PRAYER.

ST. JOHN IN PATMOS

ST. JOHN IN PATMOS, *reverse:* THE PASSION OF CHRIST.

ST. JOHN IN PATMOS, *detail:* LANDSCAPE.

ST. JOHN IN PATMOS, *detail of reverse:* CALVARY.

ST. JEROME AT PRAYER

ST. CHRISTOPHER.

THE EPIPHANY, *volets closed:* ST. GREGORY'S MASS.

THE EPIPHANY, *centre panel*

THE EPIPHANY, *volets open. Left:* THE DONOR AND ST. PETER.
*Right:* THE DONOR'S WIFE AND ST. AGNES.

86 THE EPIPHANY, *detail of centre panel:* GROUP FROM THE ADORATION.

THE EPIPHANY, *detail of centre panel:* YOUNG NEGRO ASSISTING BALTHAZAR.

88 THE EPIPHANY, *volets closed. Left volet:* ST. PETER. *Right volet:* MARY MAGDALENE.

HE EPIPHANY, *centre panel:* THE ADORATION OF THE MAGI.

THE EPIPHANY, *volets open. Left:* ST. JOSEPH. *Right:* THE SU
OF THE MAGI.

'HE CROWNING WITH THORNS.

THE CROWNING WITH THORNS

THE CROWNING WITH THORNS.

CHRIST BEFORE PILATE.

CHRIST BEFORE PILATE, *detail.*

THE CARRYING OF THE CROSS.

THE CARRYING OF THE CROSS, *detail :* VERONICA AND CHRIST.

THE TEMPTATION OF ST. ANTHONY.

THE PRODIGAL SON.

'HE PRODIGAL SON, *detail:* THE PRODIGAL.

THE PRODIGAL SON, *detail:* THE SWAN INN